For Trapped Things

For Trapped Things

Brian Kim Stefans

ROOF BOOKS
New York

The author wishes to thank the following journals and their editors for publishing portions of
this book:

Air/Light: "A Theatrical Oasis" (pts. 1-2) "It's Over," "It's Over," "Strolling on Hillhurst"

Drunken Boat: "The Men Who Sit (Les Assis)"

Fence: "Nothing but legitimate *ha ha* here," "That sweet spot between the New York School
and Guy Debord" and "The obsessions with freedom: two spaces" from "The Wild Body"
sequence

Lana Turner: "I know that some of you have probably come here for the latest," "Someday I
will be alive, and so can say those things" and "Delete the spontaneous *fuck* after a bad line"
from "The Wild Body" sequence

Poetry: "The Future is One of Place," "Ecological Poem," "To A—"

The Poetry Review (UK): "Your Book"

The Texas Review: "My Identity," "The Scaffold," "Another Serving of Potatos"

This book is made possible, in part, by the New York State
Council on the Arts with the support of Governor Kathy
Hochul and the New York State Legislature.

Roof Books
are published by
Segue Foundation
300 Bowery, New York, NY 10012
seguefoundation.com

Roof Books
are distributed by
Small Press Distribution
1341 Seventh Street
Berkeley, CA. 94710-1403
800-869-7553 or spdbooks.org

Table of Contents

Yet so tenuous, so fine
this thing is, I am
sitting on the hard bed, we could
vanish from sight like the puff
off an invisible cigarette.

—John Wieners, "Poem for Trapped Things"

Overture

for Ara Shirinyan

In the cool night of a nothing, but strangely dramatic, universe
some bookie flips through his miniature Post-its deciphering his doodles,
two women do a spacewalk and are flipped a bird by the President,
and Sweden sighs with relief as Greta Thunberg returns,

and a Feynman diagram, minding its own business, collides with a Lear jet,
and Jessye Norman retires having avoided the Apocalypse,
and somewhere over the Seychelles a CEO needs deodorant,
while America abandons the Kurds and ISIS trends on the internet,

and a pigeon on a live cam from Bryant Park poops on the shoulder of Gertrude Stein,
and the Prime Minister from Ethiopia buffs his Nobel Prize,
and Heath Ledger gives his most inscrutable, most American performance,
and a lawyer decamps to jizzicise his psyche with a massage from Jacob Epstein,

and pearl-teethed personalities argue that the dandruff on Rudy Giuliani's pate
is a fascinating *ding-an-sich* as he bromances Ukraine,
and a coupon for Chik-Fil-A tries to defang the Fourth Estate,
and the proverbial bedlamite suffers a heart attack in the *Norton Anthology*,

and opioid deaths reach a half-million in the time Big Pharma takes
to re-soil their linens, hump a trash bag, move accounts to the Islands,
and Silicon warriors man their yurts on a slope in Big Sur,
and Jonny Greenwood writes a soundtrack inspired by fracking and unicorns,

and China swarms with new gadgets, bionic mandibles, and Belt fanatics,
and Canada sits atop us, cold and tranquil as mint lozenges,
and Madagascar luxuriates in baobob leaves, and Ireland gyres for posterity,
and South Korea declares plastic surgery a national shame, though its TV serials bleed

onto the screens of most of Asia, and elsewhere (for instance, Nigeria),
and Hungary turns right, like the Philippines, and Brunei takes to stones
to punish its "deviants," men who love men, and women who love women,
and endless choirs of syco-bordinates struggle to sing in key in our relative Parliaments,

—on this cool night: I have a pork chop, peas, and English muffin for dinner,
and hearing it's Rimbaud's birthday from Jennifer Moxley on Facebook,
I don't think the gods are with us. I open my iPhone—loveless
my cats shoot shit out of their damn boxes, but will return to me, in bed.

Ecological Poem

Around the pool the hippos drool
as if the chloride wouldn't kill them.
In fact, they like to play the fool,
the harbinger, the pilgrim.

The bird that plops into the glass
makes a sound, then isn't there.
Spiders toss, in oleaginous mass,
Goo Gone into the air.

The ants that drag a beat up car
onto the lawn are emissaries
of some forgotten prince or czar
from an HBO miniseries.

The cheetah, panther, jaguar and lynx
(some of these might be the same)
conjure images of Sphinx
and other trademarked names.

The dynamited hole now teems
with insects shiny and obscene,
crawling, dying, though it dreams
an ectoplasm of green.

My own two cats stiffen, confused
at this profusion past the door.
They bat at things they've often used
for sound therapy before.

I tell you this out of principle:
that spiraling around a theme
(while naming lots of animals)
can supercharge a meme.

My own skin founders in the rush
of allergenic, if cautious, beasts.
Eyes eye darkness, ears hear hush—
the assassin's humor feasts.

Torso

Sonst könnte nicht der Bug
der Brust dich blenden
—Rilke

If the stark outline of an inscrutable torso
against an egg-blue sky is meaningful,
it's because the suffering eye was vulnerable
to its meeting of triangles, its proportions.

If that regnant statue was the cause
of viral palpitations among the commonwealth,
the rigor mortis of the stiff muscles
quickening the nerves of the provincial—

if that's all it takes—to advertise health,
like a gnat trafficking in untold wealth
of fertilized eggs, with pastures for depositing,
weeks later spawning master generations—

then of course the species will fall, imbecile,
disdaining the stratagem of variation.

Robinson–Particles

1. AS CAPITAL

As capital
mansplains the syzygy

first the right
paw, then

the left, into
the pit

of the empty
[insert name of

international finance
institution

here], we bask
in something like

freshness,
largely discursive

with the exception
of riots,

cops and ISIS.
And we must love

two horizons,
neither "represented"

by people but as
idols

of absence,
extolling the plateaus

of control and liberty,
damage and health,

boredom and *esprit*
—of something like classes

and something
like hope

resilient in the compromise
of barely being

human.
Atoms

swerve
and blossom into laces

of comfort
ensconced

in impressive shapes
assured that recursion

always implies structure,
meaning:

the atom is fixed
in an imitation future

the eternal found
in a repeatable function

even as the party
dies.

By which I mean ideology
offers a counter

to the banal,
grants a plot

to a life merely moments.
One could

be
a mere commodity

and trace the way
vacancy begets anger

and sacrifice of the few
truly human virtues:

empathy, faith,
and love.

This isn't new
and has its promise.

A god
doing a rhythmic trick

to get you into
his church:

a go
at the golden

ring inspires
a greater aspiration:

a code
emerges that unites

and offers
a family:

to be penitent
clears the eyes

of values
in things:

a history
shows poetry

and a language to
be used

by the aspirant
to transcend

mere sport
of the spiritual:

a pope
of any flavor

authors the manifesto
in time:

flavors are discovered
for the unique

cuisine of the cult
grown from sand:

the feds
step in

to suppress it
and find empty seats

as does
the television crew

—this is an homage
to Malcom X,

whatever you believe in.
No happy medium.

No parties to abhor
just the fact

of imminent confusion,
likely, recursion

into elegant failure.

2. A LIVING ROOM

A living room
becomes a nation

the moment
it is no longer a salon,

the language yet
shared.

These are notes
for a white revolution.

Like Whitman,
but:

free their doors
from the jambs

where we won't live
for self-segregation

(but really,
because it's boring).

The virtual,
properly authored

for Verso,
enlivens debate

you can overhear
with the proper

inscrutable argot
(and Amazon credit)

though agreeing
quite a lot

also helps.
And

stoning a few heretics
white enough to stone.

These are notes
for a *petite mort*

sure to shore
cred in the academies

(jets, dossiers,
off-grid accounts)

where
abstractions

banter like solids
and essences

subtract from the light
of appearances

in a gnostic
disconfirmation:

that they're all white.

3. Poems are enchanting

Poems are enchanting
like Speer's
columns of light
at Nuremberg
—they say nothing
but liberate the sky
from oppressive ground
(what they were made to serve)

betraying
gravity
even as they confirm it
not off in some afterlife, or credo
but, point by
point
soiled with the barbarity
of what we've made the world.

Merely light
flecked with crystals
of dust
in gallant arrangements
waiting
perhaps, for the soul
to animate its intricacies
and rescue it from

the simple privilege
of being better than us.
Thus, my space
to complain
doesn't place me *above*
in some television plane, some
feed, stream
or newspaper calendar:

I sit, stamp
curse like a sailor
and declare myself an opponent of
the mechanism,
dressed for war
but with a priest's disinterest,
one distended eye
leaning toward infinity.

4. Let you be informed

Let you be informed
this funny business

of flipping our names
over, discovering

worms underneath them
and some swirling staircase

descending to promise
of obscene futures

in love, in plenty
this mutual play weakness,

conjuring of depths
from surface—names

we drunkenly exchange
like a paranoid's tennis—

verges on a pathological
see-what-the-leaves-tell-us,

stranding
us

shy despite the practice
before a live studio audience.

5. He opens his

He opens his
mouth:
he's not smart.

Stays in key,
plastic
ukelele

a significant
prop, light
enough to

carry,
his cut
just right.

But who
can say: he's
slurring,

melody
moving the
lips, his

auditors "swaying
like harvest
wheat" (Auden)

—he's not
trying, and
trying too hard

to die.
It'll
all be

"captured," launched
on Youtube,
—it'll all

be all right—
no cash on
site.

He's
purring (cats
trend)

plans a death
in hollyhocks,
but has

shelter for the night.

6. Do you make movies?

Do you make movies?
Yes, I do

but grow to the regret them
the moment

they are shown
because they're done.

Why show them again?
Does one die and live again?

I think
not. A different

audience is not different
but an afterlife,

shadow of
the initial interaction,

the contract that
emerged from tensions

once
obtained.

Such is the moment:
congealing into an object

that which stands
against mere relation,

its core
the void from which emerges

the never-asked question.
It's not

a movie one makes,
merely what one discovers

in the strictness
of time

doled out by fancy images,
the illusion of trust in the foliage

of sound—that crisis.
Every later on is not equal, and

shorn to TV
or digital reductions,

my film gives up
its vital elocutions.

It becomes language.
That's never very important.

7. One dimple

One dimple
in a smile

is quite enough.
I can't see

the asymmetry,
and like it lots.

That's money
on TV,

that's the draw:
the line of the

jaw, the relations
just off.

One looks
again at that:

an *allure*.
One tries to

punch it, and
it just snaps

into seduction,
into song.

That's just form:
on film,

a steady whack
on the cell,

and,
when drawn, a gift

of the hand.
We like it well.

It hangs well
in the home:

safe violence.
It's like money:

never still,
one takes a bite

and suffers.
It's not like a wall,

it's not like a cell.
It's off,

always off,
but, again, there.

If you have it,
go to hell.

Easy money.
I'd do it, but

for fear of
the grotesque,

the tyro's grimace.
Better to have it

gifted, to
have by birth

that asymmetry
that pulls it in,

that seems like earth.
Wear it well.

8. Do not be discouraged

Do not be discouraged
with my receding form,
it argues for the ocean
and a place to go,
my paying attention
to what is beyond us
an urge for protection
not just for me, but for us.

I give you this ghost:
when I'm not with us,
it won't make you
wake
with hands upon you,
it's no video of us
enjoying some tempest
of argument, or sex.

It's a room
with a motion, like a ship
cradled in a milky,
vertiginous ocean,
drifting beyond the
economy of purpose,
    —a womb, an artifact
of a brief time of attention.

This beneficent
humble brag
warms to communion
with the social immanence
of the post-democratic,
our respect for
atoms—even as the shapes they take
are crabbily determinant.

Unfurled with the decency
and ritual fact
of a mathematical proof,
mirroring that which
moves,
while voiding the proposition,
but unable to cross the distances
to the union

—shimmering in pigments
or pixels,
wide to receive whatever
sympathy hands will grant them,
these fevers run merely
seconds,
upsetting the furniture
that comes to define them, and

hopefully, much else.
In such a cursed
imaginary,
untouched by the breath
of iconic fate—trivial, in
fact, you will walk
till you turn to this very page
that turns to you, as you fail to get older.

9. I'm kind of

I'm kind of
losing it,

losing the right
to time. If

I be the slow lane
of some angel's

flight, its
low theory,

fat mired besides
greaseless

light,
I think it not right

to persist
affixed like this

(t-shirt, income,
friendships, broken

or otherwise,
cats, texts, and hips)

a mere affront
to "speed

tending toward the infinite"
(Deleuze).

Yet,
there is no space

to complain
quite like this

field
where cosmos and chaos

meet
easily, even if

warring
—somehow the same *esprit*

governs as immanent
relations among the values

like Maxwells's
demon

run roughshod over
the carbon-based soul

keeping the teams apart
as a sort of heterologic pinball,

illustrative
but not editorial.

All aspires
to singularity,

devices that
tell time, to being

unassimilable,
arguing for

an Emperor Space (in
Wyndham Lewis's

"theological science
fiction") over

the mind-
flux,

even as you
spurn its functions.

Slowly, but at
a price, I

plant a word
in voluble

memory.
It humiliates me

again and
again: no care

for who's there
—*autres,* cams—

and so falter in the purely
human

as these rosy goggles
fixate on the

mundane, enlivening it
foolishly, for an enchantment

even in the
photo albums

competing in the distance,
images of the *I am* and *we are*

requesting
nomination.

Though I
aspire

to a book, like
Mallarmé dreamed

of,
pregnant

with Abyss,
disappointment arises

when my pasts
don't cut

it:
weak form,

meters by metronome,
clichés, goings on

about gardens
of succulents,

simplistic views on labor,
race, and

God.
Baroque with nothing,

bark
of insides,

size
of a pea—

no vocabulary
erupts

merely
pulses

of intent:
syntax.

I
cry,

shift
into lower

gear,
hope

some humor
rises to

act as ballast,
deem it a mere stretch,

as I do,
violent in time.

10. Never try, then

Never try, then
try harder.

The doxa of economy
versus the plug

on excess.

Never plug a guest,
never harden

the art. Steer,
my little cybernaut,

into harm.

My Identity

1.

I'd like to take a stand about my identity.
I'd like to be half Asian and half white.
I'd like to do that—I'd have awesome self-confidence!

2.

The sun would breathe in my Instagram photos,
saturated reds and oranges like an Italian sorbet
—Zarathustra dawns and Machiavellian twilights!

3.

I'd like to sing this native song—I'd like to know the words!
With a melody by Debussy, lyrics by Genet,
this anthem would unfurl over the hills and plains.

4.

I'd like to retreat—retreat into my identity.
I'd like never to speak, just speak when I'm meant.
I'd like to be race loyal—I'd like to sign the document.

5.

I mean it—that I really *mean* this country,
the one that is half Asian and half white,
the one between Mongolia and the local In-n-Out.

6.

I'd like to be fit with tight black jeans
to ensure procreation of my impetuous race,
the one known for poetry, the one known for trade.

7.

I'd like the world to know that I own my body,
the one appropriated by the artistic elite,
the one never painted—impossibly naked.

8.

I'd like to marry ladies who are just like me,
just one, of course, but I'd like to have to pick
between those who were born here, and those who are fake.

9.

I'd like to have a border, colorful native costumes
worn only on the holidays—I'd like to have holidays
where we commemorate famines, drink alcohols from ancient grains.

10.

I'd like to have a President who looks like me.
I'd like to have a movie star (from my race) who tells my story.
I'd like to sleep deeply—and dream only of my race.

11.

I'd like to know if my literature is up to grade,
that the literature of my race is being read,
that the literature is being written with pen and ink.

12.

I want to fight the powers, the powers that be
who crush me with their platitudes and urges to cede,
to flee and be lessened—to give up the territory.

13.

I'd like to be a missile in a missile test
and trace a glowing arc in the illiberal sky
that grants me identity, intent, and a place to cry.

14.

I'd like to take a stand about my identity.
I'd like to be half Asian and half white.
I'd like to sail on a milky sea—and eat kimchi.

15.

The quail would fall into my lap when I wasn't even aiming.
Gold records for songs I never sang would adorn my home.
I'd have the forearms of Rambo but never fight in Vietnam.

16.

I'd like to find a home for my damn country
over sixteen blocks of storefronts in LA county
with restaurants half Asian, half white—only foods I like.

17.

I'd like to be funny—I'd like to tell jokes
only half Asians would pee in their pants about,
and half white Asians would know by heart—like Arirang!

18.

I'd like to know the authenticity of this leather hide,
to have a league of peers with a similar discrepancy,
not exactly like mine, perhaps, but using it for a template.

19.

Yes, that was then, black was white, I'd proffer.
Yes, I could talk, but talk better now with words
handed down to me by centuries of sacrosanct ancestors.

20.

I'd like to be a coin in a pop up economy,
a coin unwavering in the thrill ride of history,
of X value one day, the same X value the next—and the next!

21.

I want to dance—I love to dance—and dance within me.
I don't want to dance in couples, when it's just me.
I want to dance the native dance—I love that country.

22.

I want to be the superhero of my identity.

I'd like to know if the other side is trying to screw me.

I'd like to know if the water I drink is pure for me—that I am pure.

A Theatrical Oasis in the Spine of the Moon
Or, The Deep State

for Tim Davis

1 /

This is the intelligence plan: defrosting a chicken
from Trader Joe's. Yesterday's string beans and weepy
arugula. This plan might sound like cooking
to the uninitiated. Such a conclusion would be naive:

—There is a "deep state" browning the salad leaves,
perhaps bacteria, perhaps Schopenhauer's *Willen*,
and only my soft mania grants me confidence
in my culinary superpowers: that this plan might succeed.

I've long been abandoned by the chorus of angels.
Pegah doesn't speak to me; she's "trying to get her shit together."
We've all been subtracted to our regular hells.

I've just bought a cheap bottle of wine and cigarettes.
But the World turns—the "deep state" thickens,
mocking my arugula and my pesto-choked chicken.

2 /

The cat claws the leather of my newish Ikea sofa.
My shouts of "stop it!" don't fall like a god's thunder.
My air conditioner hums. My only music
is something by Alvin Curran from a Santa Cruz experiment

—a thin wire slung taught across the campus (that's how
I remember it) granting us a "deep state" access.
The news presses on: there's turmoil in the Capital,
the king might be dethroned, but there's no chance of a cure—

some bureaucrats might retire, some simply live on
with book deals and paternosters, ripe with confession.
None of them will admit to killing my chicken,

oxidizing my string beans for the sake of the Virgin,
and will circulate among the Sunday news shows, reeking of piety,
the bottle of wine near over, Pegah still not talking,

3 /

I love a tawdry joke, and if I'm fired for one, *c'est la vie,*
so long as it is musical, and has some relation to the human.
Jokes are jokes, and if they are truly human comedy,
the tune jams the populace, though the next day is pedestrian.

Richard Pryor was great at this, and so was George Carlin.
Lenny Bruce was the martyr, like the Christ crucified,
but never in a Mel Gibson flick—he was simply the unwitting agent
who'd led the calvary. He expired on his kitchen tiles.

You saw the photos. A Jew who thought he could beat the government.
Now, the battle call has been adopted by the President.
Half the nation is impotent, another has been conscripted,

enduringly indigent—and now post bounties against the Federal?
Some illiterate turkey can raise his talons in Kentucky.
Give us a few decisions, and the States will turn the other way.

4 /

I want to freeze in my Speedo—I want my balls to freeze
amidst the scarlet eyes of Southern California fires,
Malibu basking in the air of billionaire ease
as residential Camelots tumble into virtuous, if disbelieving, seas.

And the man they call the "Skipper" because of his resemblance to Alan Hale,
(he played the "Skipper" on Gilligan's Isle) tugs at his belt,
preparing to hit me over the Speedo with his Greek fisherman's cap
only to stumble over his yacht's charred mast,

and the tea-stirrers (they are not Teamsters) lift a regnant pinkie,
like Lovey did when she got cerebral with Mr. Howell
or Gilligan, who was wearing a Speedo just like me.

I hanker for the Love of the deep state's reservoir,
the one that holds the water that could have saved Alan Hale's yacht
or a few smooth pulses from Fruity Loops' impossible DAW.

5 /

New York poets still want to be Frank O'Hara! I want to be Emma Stone,
one second the blonde vixen, another a Picasso neurotic,
in thirty seconds saving a film, like the execrable *La La Land*
and elsewhere conjuring a master class from the Billie Jean King biopic.

We loves you, Emma Stone—though you're not helping me to die slower,
to sink into the mattress-in-a-box, to trust in therapy
for my Thor "temporarily disenfranchised" in a mental trailer
—you've got me thumbing the ropes, like that elegant fish, Peter Lorre.

But back to Gena Rowlands, who was never in a Frank O'Hara movie,
since movies have foundered since Will Smith got de-aged
by Ang Lee in a flick I passed on, much as I loved *Crouching Tiger, Hidden Dragon,*

with its "message from afar" that I inflict on my screenplay students.
Hélas, New York: time to bathe in the froufrou on the wifi,
refill the revolutionary slow cooker, and indulge in Paleolithic diets.

6 /

Hard to say "democratic"—there are no "votes" on the streets of Thai Town,
few here hold opinions about the new tariffs against Hong Kong,
no one's watching Chuck Todd in the warm hearths of their tent encampments
that appear and disappear, like England's Roman settlements

—but in days, not centuries. I don't know what sort of kibitzing happens
in white Protestant enclaves in Montana or Michigan,
and concur that it's a blindness—I haven't met the inhabitants
of the non-coastal *states*, Democrats or Republicans.

But I hear a Syrian expostulate into his phone about locally-made croissants
and the probiotic drink he's carrying, while that handsome Mongolian
draws out a plastic bag for me (though I bring my own,

—I'm sort of a white liberal that way) to pack up my obscenities.
I'm not the Korean *singularity*. I'm an atom with an Instagram.
I've just bought a pack of cigarettes, and crossed several continents.

7 /

The cat rubs more love goo on my bouncing knee.
Quite a gambit for attraction, but he's barely seventeen.
Outside, on the cops, are imitation leather,
some jaundiced donuts, tires with conspiring treads.

The journalists of the *Guardian* are writing—ours
are channeling, a mere circumstance of the World's turning.
We wait for the text. All the clashing *Willen*
chymify themselves, unaccounted beneath the bylines.

We can only hope that this poem might be pretty,
melody that darts across the bureaucracies of intention,
a Sprite in peripheral vision, balletic, *seizing*

and promising, above the sprawl, the image of a City.
Facts and re-facts and un-facts conspire to deceive.
An ambulance and a chihuahua howl in the distant gray.

8 /

The circle of a bicycle tire is the cover of a Germs album.
A slice of "cheese pizza" has become a symbol for child pornography
(look that one up, but—trigger warning—it's not "random,"
but something like Exhibit A of the deep state's shoulder claw on humanity).

I'm not going to look that up. I'm inured to the Google mind meld
that made quick work of the memorable family squabbles
about whether the Police, the Cars, or the Go-Go's were the balls,
or whether the Rangers could ever beat the Devils.

I'll be a counter-revolutionary as the bile drip drips slower,
sing the singe of my causal wires, cancel my subscriptions,
my neuralgia, my Sisyphus, my phenomenal mass-thought from Heidegger,

and bungle like a neon rabbit while not channelling Henry Miller.
The genius behind the genius of *Brokeback Mountain* (I've changed the subject)
brought it to the point—that Love is a white shirt in a closet.

9 /

That's my inner dialogue: I twitch beyond obvious righteousness,
—the vote for progressives, the vote for the free market—
angling like a Watt-figure among the wheelchairs and tents
wondering if, outside of "justice," I'd get a 10 for my performance.

There are many others I could conjure, though it's raining men
when the earth explodes with zingers, like dandelions
(though we don't have dandelions in L.A.), or like rains from El Niño,
that pelt the dust and over-rated succulents of Runyon Canyon.

Yes, this all sounds pretty cool—a way to Zorro with panache
the zombilly unimaginative when they conspire in enmity,
the ones addicted to Paradise gas, for whom shitting is not entropy,

the ones who wake impossibly confirmed, in a data-czar's employ.
Verlaine wrote: *Fuck rhetoric*—in a teacup of perfect rhyme,
a dime of quietness, of comforting heresy, of Love beyond time.

10 /

Perhaps the study of happiness that no one eludes
has camped under my feet, licking his paws.
There's a lot of clap-trapping clogging up the news.
The cat finds solace sharpening his claws,

signaling his defiance of basic physical laws:
cats don't watch news. I'd like not to,
too. I'd rather watch Billie Eilish stretching her jaws
on *Saturday Night Live* while dancing on the roof.

But what about the *poem*—is it really so floozy easy,
a Thursday night date with booze and cigarettes
in a Neo-realist film budgeted "B," starring

a paper maché eggplant, and a tumescent high school athlete?
I like breathing—no problem granting it words.
If the breath won't lie in bed with me, I'm sure it cares.

11 /

The armies are marching, marching—on the internet!
The martial Tweets and mercenary Facebook posts are at the gates
of the Capital! We've raised our cameras and scythes,
and are turning animal! Blood will spill, and at a high bitrate!

Stories from *The Hill* and *Politico* will heat our pulse!
We'll fight for better news anchors, who cares about Shepard Smith!
We'll tear them down, no better than ventriloquists!
Kimmel and Colbert will be our Jeanne d'Arcs—our Vulgarians!

We'll never have to leave the comforts of our evening hosts,
the tracings of the "rational" a heart-warming placebo,
as the galumphing tactics of a hotel-emolument Nationalist

—Fascist, whatevs—pull rabbits from our Constitutional aporias!
You are not "leftist" because you're "liberal"—dissociate this couplet.
What falls at the feet of the "voter" are golden apples.

12 /

The deep state has no patience for bourgeois solace:
it bubbles in the decaying pipes of the waterways in Michigan,
it pulses in the packets of liquor store ramen,
it kills the scallop and sea turtle in the Pacific Ocean,

it levels its salty tear on the most adventurous vacations,
the trek to Machu Picchu, Nashville, or Vons—
I listen to the deep state for my next dalliance
and wonder: Who's had butterflies hatch in their beard?

Who's traced a curve and called it "Bird in Space"?
Who's had a sixth finger emerge while they're painting?
Who's had their vision reduced to six primary

colors—lines rectilinear, and the diagonal a heresy?
The *true stroke* still has value, ephemeral as it is,
and falling into the abyss, grasping, is extreme sporting.

13 /

The Seventies tried your game—the punks turned mortality
into extravagant travesty, and the poets were popping quaaludes,
—but now we want it *all*, a paradigm for the eternal,
a promise of endless life, while sitting on the Mice that Roar:

sex until you're eighty, grandchildren in droves who mewl
until they're part of Democracy, but who don't learn more than to survive,
as the Knack throbs their song about the "teenage sort,"
and a girl smokes bubblegum Camels through unkempt tonsils.

Dying ever slower: it's counter-revolutionary. The gut sags
but there's a pill for that—a plan for that—with siliconed geriatrics,
the bile dropping in a slow drip into the potted plants,

and any show of *dis-ease* just fanatical, Sanders-esque theatrics.
The deep state quickens as it finds its compass—Xanax—
and keeps us from the brink, a null distance from our pickaxes.

14 /

This is the temptation: to fuck around with the iPhone,
free synthesizer apps with dark, sexy interfaces,
wheel between the sine and the square waves, master a drone
worthy of Terry Riley, La Monte Young, or John Cale.

A lossless afternoon. Something like this can account for non-reading,
sounding the inner dome with synaptic susurrus,
—the Old Men of Haddam, reeking of feathers, reclining
in symbolical spaces, but never sounding assurances.

The inner ear and the slave to the virtual are not much
different. The former has legends and bacchanals,
fevers and sense, lost causes at distance, the World held in abeyance.

The latter is titillation: pulchritudinous mathematics
descended from the eternal to argue its aesthetic
verities. A mosquito laps at the ear, and will soon be dead.

15 /

Everyone wakes up, fragrant with new developments, vexed in their fields
of attractions, chasing Baudelairean cats down the hallways
of this repurposed mental hospital, not sure if the World is still on stilts
crossing the Andalusian Sea on its way to Norway

to meet wise people, get free health care, and photograph the fjords
and otherwise bask in our post-Pangean interlude of being stable.
Youth has gotten so fancy in this economic downturn,
if by "downturn" we mean the inching forward of tele-surveillance Capital,

shaved sides and purple combovers, tattered jeans and turntables
to keep them tied to the analog, to feel the "Bern,"
Phoebe Waller-Bridge as the new Secretary of Education

LARPing adventures in the Andes with characters from A.A. Milne,
happy hours in the Castle Wirtemberg, and a cornucopia of commandments
moving sometimes to the right, to the left, like cardigans.

16 /

I want to fall out of love with this deep state, not that they're asking
for my paw on the dotted line, my grease on the contract
—they leave me quite alone, which is a show of generosity,
or negligence, or stupidity, as I retire into my Aflac.

I wonder if the belly scratchers who populate the "debates"
are just drum circle pulsers, instinctive, prelapsarian,
fodder for the data sluts, or a protein rush in my Ovaltine,
and I should just listen more closely to the Bay Area communists.

Perhaps the study of happiness that no one eludes
is gripping a *Watchtower* while sounding my doorbell's Beethoven,
or is the Scientologist needling me at La Poubelle

who is writing a book of conspiracy theories about Olivia Colman
or is the inventor of the "Green Super Drink" they sell at Trader Joe's
or is the latest kitten to adopt me at Saint D'ore.

17 /

I certainly don't think the gods are with us, Hölderlin.
I fancy I'm just a shuffling fetus who bucked the trends,
some palpitating jellyfish who took to land
hearing the wages were generous, in the world of men.

Perhaps I'd merely ascended from a deep sea vent
to put on this flesh suit—two arms, two legs, nipples and a chin—
and carry within some memory of the acids
that still animate this quizzical, humanish actant.

Oh, I would love to have a god within me. I wouldn't be lonely
shoveling into my gullet microwaved peas,
or soaping my genitals, warbling pop tunes decades old

—not from Eternity—fearing the *state* inside me,
and could fathom how there's no verdict in my credit cards,
that Man bargains with the gland, and is still of earth.

18 /

I'm getting hungry. I've emptied my bottle of wine.
My cats, supporting supplicants, are silent.
It's a quarter past strophe, much past my bedtime.
I'm loath to disappear now; I appreciate the violence

of testing thought against rash impurities,
of acting imbecilic in the perfunctory courts of stanzas,
The news no one can elude provides us narratives:
Rachel Maddow has documents, charisma, some nerve,

Sean Hannity a haircut, diuretic palliatives,
and a host of candidates their impressionistic overtures.
The deep state is *slime*, but let's trust in the "deep state"

—its form is merely intemperate agency:
the bacteria browns my arugula, what I see of the New gestates
in the gut of an extremophile as it swallows the sea.

Point and Void

The sweet-lipp'd sisters, musically frighted,
Singing their fears, are fearfully delighted
—Richard Crashaw

I'm desultory as an oil slick on the rib of a whale,
Kodachromed as an image in an ironic tale,
bled of all my sewage in a passionless confession,
powder-white as a mannequin in a boiling cauldron,

nip-and-tucked as a hieroglyph on a moldy slate,
pantomimed as a baseball jersey that is celibate,
swirled as a toxic creamer in a liver pool,
lozenged in the throat of labyrinthine drool,

paralyzed like a tortoise on the verge of remission,
diddled in the caverns of the sinking sun,
Shawshank Redemptioned inside the whites of igloos,
spun like a porcelain top among the *entre nous,*

inflated like gastric blubber in the Aerodrome,
Pancho Villaed in the Dothraki of a palindrome,
devoured by the fumes of the vanilla smokers,
gut-wrenched by the timetables of insensate Kurds,

cannibalized by cats that emote with swamp lust,
vagrantized by the Tweet blasts of Elon Musk,
skewered by the cook with the Bolshy stopwatch,
fandangoed into the crotch of a boozy Sasquatch,

pilloried like a Funyun on a Winterfell spike,
Ogden Nashed in a clutch of conqueror tykes,
whiplashed in the lottery of crustacean Reichs,
prettified as a pinwheel on a landscape of high fives,

de-orgoned as an atom in the sanatorium of Wills,
unrevised as a telegram that sporked the battles,
blustered as a bandwagon of gush in the Parliament,
Voodoo Dolled in the osteoblast in the womb of the universe,

Johny-come-latelied in the boxer's velvet thongs,
deified as the catamaran of the latest health options,
victimized by the romance of the gormless Heiress,
pin-the-tail-on-the-donkeyed by the saintly humorless,

jabberwockedly honkied by the coils of the Khan,
Forest-Gumped as a Zelig by the Kennedy assassination,
Billy-Collinsed as a tool for the latest dog repair,
unveiled as the English butler with sarcasm to spare,

loopedy-looped over the Passion Play of Cassius Clay,
Jerry Springered within the Botox of Frito Lays;
Scooby-Dooed in the wash cycles of Christian denominations,
poo-pooed by the Upper West Side's social lucubrations,

sugar-daddied among the gusts of financial calculations,
Audened among the rations of the free verse option,
unencumbered as an orphan in a Chumbawamba spree,
black-marketed in the Scots of kings that would be bees,

Nick Draked as a Kindermass of EDM'd zombies,
perfected as a hook for salmon-huffing rabies,
laugh-tracked as a Lincoln debate on CBS News,
rubber-necked as a feather duster in an apse of blue pews,

fine-and-dandied as a salaried cog in a cow market,
24-hour-labored in the featherweight class of progress,
perfected as a lemon in just a perfect lemon tree,
ungloved as Gwyneth Paltrow among nature's indecencies,

bungled as a jungle that blurts of halcyon days,
filibustered as the one who tucked St. Trafalgar's bae,
mumbled as a monody in the Kenyan commons,
Brexited as a troglodyte surviving only on bacon,

Ricardo Montalbaned by the Ciceros of denigration policy,
fêted as a thumbnail on an old Windows screen,
tawdried among the auks of the pacifically breathing,
vegatarianized among the Hogwarts of the seething eating

—but I *love*—the body moves forward. Remark its retreat
graceful as Kate Valk down a Tribeca street,
humans dissimulating sideways, eluding the provocative pliés,
the wild hugs and kisses of my teetering forays,

ignoring the point and void of my Pascalian soul
plotted here on the graph of the presumed "universal,"
brilliantined as the hair of a Bollywood idol,
sanguine on a barque beside an atom-bombed atoll.

The Men Who Sit [Les Assis]

after Arthur Rimbaud

Gashed with pocks, scabby—their eyes encircled with green
bags, chubby fingers gripping their
thighs, their skulls plated with a haughtiness, vague
as the leprous flowerings of old walls—

They are knotted in epileptic loves,
their fantastic ossatures fixed to the black skeletons
of the chairs, their feet to rachitic
stalks—they are entwined there, mornings and nights!

Old men sinking, one with their seats: the
vitamin sun makes burlap of their skin
—and, with eyes turned toward winter's falling snow,
they tremble there, like pinched toads.

But the seats are good to them: shit
brown, old straw yields to their neglected hinds.
Dying suns, swaddled in stalks
of the corn they once fermented, shine for them.

Question marks, knees in teeth, green
pianists, ten fingers rapping a tambourine under
their seats... they sway to soft barcaroles,
their scissored scalps float on these motions of love.

Oh, but what is it that makes them get up? What a shipwreck
of scolded cats! Whining, stretching
—arise more slowly, Olympic champs!
Their trousers puff around their bloated thighs.

And you can hear them: their bald heads
knock the dark walls... they stamp torqued feet,
thump after thump. Their buttons? The eyes of crouched beasts
leering from down salty corridors.

Then, they own that invisible hand
that murders: their gaze filters black poisons, cursing
the cadaverous eye of the pitiful dog,
so you choke. You are stuffed in obnoxious funnels.

Relaxed, fists plunged
in coarse cuffs—they've forgotten what made them get up!
From morning's aurora to evening, tonsils bunched
in miniature chins—nearly burst with agitations!

When a sleep lowers their eyelids...
they dream of their seats made fecund, of keen
lovers waiting in droves. They frisk among chairs to be born
amidst these proud bureaus.

Flowers of ink spit their pollen in commas
and comfort them... the length of crouched calyxes,
the flight of dragonflies by a file of gladiolas
—and the barbed ears of corn arouse their penises.

1992/2014

Poem

A secretary
at a public
high school

in Lancaster,
Pennsylvania,
said

she was pleasantly
surprised
her pay went up

$1.50
a
week.

She said
that will
more than cover her

Costco
membership
for the year.

Toy Mammal

A silver mammal, a blue mammal,
a toy mammal, a wooden mammal.
Can it be the latter two
are all there will be of the wondrous?

The battery mammal inside the plastic mammal
swimming, two by two, with mammal intelligence,
some clever AI that the CIA
hopes can deceive the Russians?

      Could it be that this, too,
      is simply wondrous?

The mammal child in the playpen
will never dream of swimming with dolphins
though that's how he learns the letter "d,"
(in the future, it will be for "Demerol"),
and finds dolphins in Pixar films
not nearly as interesting as robotics.

      He earns his twisting dolphin
      at a Black Friday sale.

The credit card mammal and the war mammal
read about Iran on the phone mammal,
the words of a raging animal
who puts American mammals first:
the prairie cougar over the desert lion,
the red squirrel over the sloth,
the Iowan over the Inuit,
the Philly cheese steak over Croatian tomatoes.

      Mammal pride comes first,
      and tomatoes are not mammals.

The child will learn that his parents aren't mammals,
even as they poked a book at the letter "d,"
they were just images on YouTube,
and even breast-feeding was an act of TV.

     Any mammal that even spoke to him
     was a preternatural mammal,

a silver mammal, or a blue mammal,
not a toy mammal, or a wooden mammal.

The Future Is One of Place

The future is one of place
devoid of race.
A jawbone under a sock
is a geological clock.

The plunking of rain
on the termite-riddled window pane:
reading a Bible on that ledge
is a tiny college.

A Galapagos tortoise is killed
(or, simply, unwilled).
The Ebola virus weeps, or retires,
because, like us, it tires.

Meanwhile, below the subbasement,
a Suede Revolution:
the phlegmatic skill of the cryptographer
soixante-huitards the teleprompter.

The id in facsimile
is suspended on a leash,
twisting in the rain
above that goddamned window pane.

Being is slightly corrupted
by the Thinking that's one-upped it
(like the pun on pain)
and will never love again.

Hot Rocks

POEM

I get so nervous
writing.

*

No time to *condensare*
like the present.
Just don't be a *dichten* about it.

*

POEM

I feel
stiff drinks.

*

SPELL CECIL

didn't fix that.

*

POLITICAL POEM

1 Read the *Tractatus* today.
1.1 Let's start a war!

*

Sent: Thursday, January 13, 2000 8:56 AM
Subject: Tapeworm

內躬偕爻,虜,齦滌`偕爻齦滌`偕爻,虜,齦滌`偕爻齦滌`偕中滌`偕

Now try to excise it from your memory.

*

ACH DU, PLAGIARISM!
Daddy, daddy, you bastard, I'm through.

*

TRAVEL POEM

No freakin' USB port.
Everybody on this flight hates me.
Not enough room for my 1 lb. bag of cashews.
A bit warm.

*

TRAVEL POEM

Glad I'm taking Cathay Pacific and not Cathay Atlantic (for this trip).
All the Japanese offerings feature a 40-something man talking on his cell phone with a GRI-
    MACE.
You have braces.
I'll have the beef provençal, green beans, carrots and parsley red bliss potato. Yes, the beef.

*

There has to be punishment.

*

THINKING BIG

"The United States cannot annihilate the Chinese nation with its small stack of atom bombs.
Even if the U.S. atom bombs were so powerful that, when dropped on China, they would
make a hole right through the earth, or even blow it up, that would hardly mean anything to
the universe as a whole, though it might be a major event for the solar system."
    —Mao Zedong, "The Chinese People Cannot Be Cowed by the Atom Bomb," 1955.

*

Bach, Beethoven, Brahms.
Bed, Bath, Beyond.

*

"That girl over there, she doesn't even know
who Žižek is. ŽIŽEK."

I smiled at him and waved.

*

3. What art movement is associated with the idea of cutting up a newspaper, putting the pieces
in a hat and pulling words and phrases out randomly to make a poem?
A. Daddy
B. Doo Doo
C. Playdoh
D. Republicanism

*

My girlfriend and I got into a bitter argument last night:
Me: Did this avocado go bad?
She: You're a puppet.
Me: No, you're a puppet.
She: YOU are the puppet!
Me: No, YOU are the puppet!
She: You're a puppet.
Me: Ha, no. You the puppet.
She: YOU... ARE... the PUPPET!
Me: No, YOU are the puppet! P-U-P-...
She: Ugh. (puppet)
Me: Don't talk under your breath at me... you... nasty woman!
And then I got pulled off the stage with the hook of a large oak cane.

*

Sanders Wins Ontario.

*

Are you there Florida? It's me, Margaret.

*

THING

"Is there any way we can screw him?" Mr. Nixon can be heard asking of Mr. Cavett.

*

THIS IS JUST TO SAY (SEPT. 26, 2016)

Today is the day
we truly take our place

among the developing countries.
Let's hope that BRIC

let's us in.

*

It's all you deserve:
a little prose.

The Rain [Pastoral]

The rain was *insanely great*, the sand was *think different*.
Palms swayed in the 2.4 Ghz wind. The cats were 4K.
The bachelorhood was abolished in a wash of *stay connected*.
The text was *don't be evil* and the author Russian.

The angels chorused in the quadrophonic speakers.
I'm unclear if they were there or preternaturally lossless.
The devils were incarnated with inscrutable CGI,
the light strictly OLED, as befits the prince of darkness.

The chairs were from a 3D printer with a 4D option.
The lover was impressive with his or her artisanal polygons,
the body Platonically holy on a 12" or 40" screen,
zapped into the room by cretins in the Bay or Ukraine.

Back at the ranch, the cows pooped into compost heaps
enriched by recycled cardboard, kale, and Omega 3.
Pigs lolled in the breezes of their carbon monoxide.
Roosters crowed in the morning, autotune corrected.

And the rain pounded loudly, insanely, differently,
on the sand acquired legally with skill and power-ups,
or accrued sketchily with an army of ninja teens
self-employed in the bivouac of sofa-supported games.

In the event of an emergency, the toilets were wifi ready
as the plane tumbled down into a high bitrate sea.
The night returned to its time zone, rebooted by Starlink,
swerving above the mattress-in-a-box, insufferably clean.

Among the Things

Among the things
I don't deserve

is this time to
write.

They call it
a civil right, this demand

that I not write.
But I

can't simply wait
much as I agree: it's pointless

this commerce
with the "far right"

on my near left
asking me to

die.
It would be funny to comply

(propitious,
environmental)

if only for a
while. Then

stage a resurrection—
author photos, fresh blurbs,

the "life"—if
only out of spite.

This time, I'll try
to be nice

—void
the propositional (anything

I might
want to say

about this or that,
flip, or snide: the

catnip of trolls
and slights

exponentially arrogated
to principle). Or not.

Daily traffic
of reviews

and "likes,"
barbiturates

of the internet,
polysyllables

of the monolettristic,
stress me

out. I'd come out
often to,

say, exercise
my right to, say, exercise

in broad daylight
if the price were

right: if they'd shut up
for the night.

Put the trash
out, call in

the cat, brush, then
shut up,

shut up and let me write.
It's boring being

dead
as the meat, the

"life"
calls me from the crypt

I've just fixed up so
nicely with

Alex Katz
prints, frames around

my rare LPs, books
of old

poetry (not
the kind

to draw me into the
fight). I

have it so
nice.

But death has its price:
nothing to which

to cling, or fog
my diamond mirror with.

Curses and banishments
come and go

with the grave, thick turns
of *Game of Thrones*

and repercussions waver
with the cinematic sheen

of Biblical epics
or Hawthorne's *Scarlet Letter*

even as
these heroes can't commit

to more than a thimbleful
of violating

prose.
But I lie:

shielding a preference
for the singular

oil
against the numerical,

a feeling I might
be wise to hide.

So let me
die for the night.

Poems Starting with a Line by Walt Whitman

1 : QUESTIONS OF CONTEXT

"I cock my hat as I please indoors or out,"
I zip up my fly but often zip it down
in formal occasions where laughter's not allowed,
but zip it back up when there's Money around.

2 : REFLECTION ON FORMS

"To be in any form, what is that?"
to be in one is difficult enough
slaying the other forms that, like tyrants,
aim to restrict the polyphony of love.

To hold fast, to simply be mortal
in the ways a newspaper applauds,
tries the wit, and tries the hairstyle,
and tries the blue jeans of the anthropoid

who otherwise might be a saurian,
or a Martian, or an antique photograph,
impossibly young, in the Earth's demesne,
waking with the genitals of Adam.

3 : WHAT IS COMMONEST

"What is commonest and cheapest and nearest and easiest is Me,"
sitting on a bar stool with the most interestedness of company
who don't want to hear of the soap opera of Language poets
being harangued on Facebook, or after the last MLA conference.

What is terrible and inevitable and infinitely depressing
is what little I have to say about theoretical musings
about the plight of the subject, about the individual and dialectics,
about the march of history in the prison-house of academics.

What is piss-stained and boiler-room and otherwise provincial
is the fuck I give for the imperial science that flattens all
and can't stand that we're here procrastinating on bar stools
while the abstractors cavil about justice, and I just want to talk.

4 : The Gang

"One of that centripetal and centrifugal gang,"
the one with the voice like a rubber band,
the one who tossed a lemon and then ran to catch it,
the one who sweated on both the inside and the outside,

was excommunicated from the aforementioned gang—
the *centripetal* claiming that he never deigned
to call when he wandered off into the Plains of the Id,
and the *centrifugal* that he was plain dim-witted.

5 : Gossip About Faith

"My faith is the greatest of faiths and the least of faiths,'"
slumming in Netflix series and Twitter rants,
commuting among the ear-bud savants, the Master-phone slaves,
hungry as a Jain passenger who won't even eat plants,

uncounted as a bacterium in the roll-call of agents
who'd vowed a pledge to China or Russia, or to the U.S. President—
the E. Coli who could flip the vote, so that humans be pathogens
in jousts in coffee shops—about impossible Justice.

My call to retreat is really about only *one* cow,
this babe who really drinks too much, unlike the old gray bard,
much as love bubbles among side-burned journalists
who awaken each morning refreshed, recovering from hangovers—

the one that *I* have, swiping, disconsolate, the iPhone
—*they* might be athletes of facts, but I'm data-depression prone—
so I retire into my pajamas, riddled with kitty scat,
hopeful that the *poem*—this Phone Home of type—can Roomba that.

6 : The Martyrs

"The disdain and calmness of martyrs,"
mascaraed eyes on Rodeo Boulevard
in the nineteen-seventies; the solace of rappers
unwinding rhymes in Compton or Watts;

the slug-like gaze of the parentally abandoned
from Oregon or Washington, pierced, with their guard dogs,
slumming for a chiclet of change,
with paradisal passions, nursing wounds;

the unfortunate dolphin, swimming in an ocean
yearly corrupted with plastic beads;
the woman who can only look back on rape,
on humiliations, on disease—though she's pure;

the immigrant who believed in his State,
a linguistic one, and bragging of culture
signifying the birth of a nation—*that* was poetry—
all left behind for a food cart;

the African country, one of many,
a territory ringing a gaggle of tribes and religions,
that aspires, ironically, for the Western yoke
that delegates through "democratic" parties;

the child who watches her tenders throw dishes;
the gloomy deities of domestic qualms;
those courting language from the universe
in dribs and drabs—might have written this poem.

7 : Reflections on Impeachment

"Be at peace bloody flukes of doubters and sullen mopers,"
basketball fans at Shrimp Lover's, *Deep Space Nine* fans on the couch,
be a part of the *ohm*, the media swirl of impeachment,
the chemical farm of the ant swarm, the river gods of sewers.

Plug yourself into Wakefulness training, you blue Cinderellas
scrubbing the floors at the Chateau Marmont with your heels and taffetas,
tune out to tune into the late night show hosts,
as the rubber slug of impeachment wends along the coasts.

There was fire in the capital in 1793
—the capital of France, that is—an eloquent beheading,
the flukes of doubters and sullen mopers having arisen from lethargy,
over-caffeinated morning news junkies, quick studies of the martial.

Such clouds surround us! But they're filled with drones and fighter jets,
satellites from China and Elon Musk, not gods in Parnassus
—Zeus has turned to real estate, Athena's a YouTube sensation—
and first-person shooters have gamified the Bastille.

No thunder will come from gods—we're Marvel Studios plebeians,
a new season every summer, a new series every month,
and the *rebel god*—Milton did a pretty good job with Satan—
will not rise to grease the wheels of impeachment proceedings.

So microwave your popcorn, shovel the turds from your kitty litter,
be at peace, bloody flukes of doubters and sullen mopers!
Awesome television is at hand! But not the awful paradigm shift
that brings the poor into Eden—the one on the teleprompter.

8 : THOUGHT

"I am the poet of the woman same as the man"
which is difficult, since I can't understand
what makes a man a woman, and a woman a man,
since women are all poets, and men aspirants.

Los Angeles Portrait: Bus Stop

Waiting for the bus on Sunset
and Normandie—a small cast
of Latinas, chattering or silent,
who got there before me, aristocrats
of the shuffling majority
who wax and buff the automobiles
of the Beverly Hills, impossibly wealthy,
and return at five, standing in the aisles—

or a homeless man—glowering, or sick?—
 my sole partner on the green bench
(this not being rush hour), hearing music
that only pulses his dry head,
sometimes groomed, sometimes unhygienic,
and sometimes I offer him a sandwich
which he accepts—it's wrapped in plastic,
a corner store chicken salad I'd bought for lunch—

or a young model (this being Los Angeles),
with baroque tattoos that seem
to me, who doesn't know the business,
to narrow the range of her shoot's personae—
no nymph-in-the-woods type,
no Swiss Miss, rather an MTV
vamp goddess from the 80s, or what Vice
prophesied would be the new standard of beauty—

or a student, this being the line
 from Hollywood to UCLA,
ear buds, eyes fixed on a phone,
as if talking were déclassé,
as if seeing and hearing in three dimensions
was nothing but a botched video game,
an *umwelt* to be suffered for seconds
when the charger had been misplaced—

or someone we might call "random"
—a woman whispering to herself
in Spanish some Christian psalm
—a stumbling club-goer, still half-
drunk from a bludgeoned 4 AM
—a young man of color in a suit
rehearsing his resume and stratagem
—a Kurdish math genius (long story, but true)

—all of them!
    But here's where it gets ugly:
it could just be me, unshaven,
groggy from last night's wine, feebly
pretending my clothes fit, my gut's not bulging,
 tugging a lecture from fogged memory
so my students don't think I'm a French decadent,
or a hapless casualty of ADHD
who *scans* homework that needs close attention—

an insuperable me, pea of the universe,
no giant, no Whitmanic cosmos,
happy that I won't have to use quarters
since I remembered to refill my bus pass,
happy to have given the sandwich
to the homeless man, another stray atom,
unread by the agora, dark in the dark passage
between birth and death—and new as Adam.

To A—

Thinking.
Wondering if
my trot to Paris
to suffer you
wasn't all wrong.
My *amour fou*

precise as a shark
collecting scents
miles off,
exact as a saint
cowed before
invisible wings

rustling
abstract sheets?
Your eyes
green, and red
your hair
iconic in this

television universe
of one man
let nothing on,
no "real"Twitter feed
surrendering candid
portraits of what

you believe,
what you love.
And I sit, subtracted,
before my love.
Wondering.
Subjected

as I was
to plural echoes
nth parts sensual,
nth parts trust,
and to hear there
a call

to illegitimate Paris
where I fit
right in,
Jacques Brel songbook,
ukulele, bread
and wine, simulacral

maudit bohemian
pelted by Polanski-ish
rain, but happy
away from Los Angeles
where you fit in
being able, in one city

to drive for hours
and never leave home.
My choked voice grumbled
"les chrysanthèmes"
(Brel song) as
I sought the streets

of Apollinaire's "Zone"
on Google maps
(which I paid dearly
for)
still hearing the
angel

even as
you were angry with me
who nearly destroyed
your apartment's electricity

plugging in some idiotic
gadget of mine

and leaving it smoking
drunk on uke, bread and wine.
Hard not to think
this symbolic
or a great way to pep
up an episode

of "Friends," or an ancient
Merchant Ivory film.
If I were Anne Carson
you'd be translation
and I
an impotent scholar

before the Greek,
drawn by love
to the undecided
omnivorous Word
that paints travelogue,
that shields earth,

begging
this word *side with me*
when I touch down in Paris,
that it's you who'd ground
this polysemous
text

with a kiss, or touch
puppyish, unambiguous.
Oh, that Anne
Carson, such a genius.
She makes
me think.

I've never been
so wrong, and in
the wrong place,
a foreigner, foreigned
in my own goddamned
country

by double negation
fitting right
in (as I've
said) and you
a Mediterranean accent
amidst the stones

of French abstraction,
pride, often cruelty,
noir desirs
circling like bats
who've read too much Saint-Just
and mistaken it for Sade.

(That sounds quite important.
I'm afraid it's not.)
It rained. I wrote
a pining song
in a hotel room
refusing your offer

to stay with you
and your boyfriend
(*quelle horreur*)
who spoke no French
while I
conducted vertiginous conversations

with a curator
at the Musée Gustave Moreau
pinning my hopes
on words like "Gautier" (Théophile)

"Mallarmé" and "Rimbaud"
(who didn't come up

of course),
and marred the language
even further with the help
of Google translate
in my letters to you
in the guise of, who?

it wasn't Baudelaire
(I can't remember who,
maybe Marat,
and you, Charlotte Corday).
I liked the pining song,
in the end,

it's Morrissey-esque, funny
but grim, slippery
and only incomplete
without (or with) you.
Here I do not
go again,

merely think
flat footed
on my horizon
(scratching
my itchy head, I
think I have dandruff)

while you
sleep
in a Westwood AirBnB
lyrically, so
I am drawn
shark-angelly

down Hollywood Blvd.
on the 302
to an American-style
aperitivo
with sliders instead
of funicular olives

again with you
talking,
and I gazing deep
into your colors
reading your Tweets
but never commenting.

Such lovely olives.
It's a beautiful evening.

The Arboretum

starting with a line by Walt Whitman

for John Ashbery

"Blind loving wrestling touch," we're here in the arboretum
drinking wine from paper cups, our car keys in a soap dish,
the weather pale and ginger and not offering us much
to say about it—about how the mordant scuttlebutt
of the Legions ruling over us
don't have the character of gods—we stare into our boxed liquors,
flip through Curious George, raise our arms to rhythms
barely heard in the arboretum, and do not ask for much
but for this Sunday's company.

Could it be the genius of the sky was a rumor?
That the wind lashing the slats was merely pre-recorded,
hale that cracked the glass door, screwed the antennae up,
was some demonic Mister, a talk show host, perhaps,
pining for daily ratings,
hurling phlegmatic zingers in lathered balls of spit
upon the roof of the arboretum? Could it be the whirring leaves
were a CGI holograph, and us just Xbox subscribers?
(I ask, and reach for a scotch.)

The crowd is growing thinner, some have already tossed their cups,
the paradise long ended of some *blind loving touch*
emerging from conversations that always turned to wrestling,
the sharp thrust of a hand up into the armpit, or an arm
around the vein-distended neck
to toss the body down. That was all just speculation,
in fact, we exchanged numbers for a later celebration—
this time with cheese and crackers, and, loving us, the gods
in a dedicated transmission.

Russia

It is clear that the world is purely parodic
—Georges Bataille

after Allen Ginsberg's "America"

Russia I've given you all and now I'm nothing.
Russia a Netflix subscription, a respectable credit rating and my way around BitTorrent,
    January 10th, 2017.
I can't stand my own water.
Russia when will we end the human war?
Go fuck yourself with your American Presidents and legions of *NY Times* trolls.
I don't feel good don't hack me.
(Ok, hack me.)
I won't write my poem till I'm in Ann Coulter's right mind.
Russia when will you be autotelic?
When will you take off my Reeboks?
When will you look at yourself through the prism of *Deep Space Nine*?
When will you be worthy of your million Michelle Obama fans?
Russia why are your libraries full of copyright infringements?
Russia when will you send your kale to Big Sur?
Your cell phones to Nigeria?
I'm sick of your jock-like demands.
When can I go into the supermarket and buy what I need with the bare fact of my American
    citizenship?
Russia after all it is you and I who are perfect not the Ukrainians.
Your democracy is too much for me.
You made me want to be a saint (or a Korean).
There must be some other way to settle this Facebook thread.
Assange is in Ecuador I don't think he'll come back (it's fine).
Are you in Ecuador or is this some form of practical joke?
I'm trying to write a sonnet.
Russia I feel sentimental about Creedence Clearwater Revival and Viktor Tsoi.
Russia I used to be a Jedi when I was a kid and I'm not sorry.
I eat kale every chance I get.
When I go to Chinatown I get drunk but you get laid.
My mind is made up there's going to be Marx.

My psychoanalyst thinks I'm the Lord's Prayer.

I have mystical visions and cosmic vibrations and I still haven't told you what you did to
SpongeBob SquarePants after he got his hair sporked on Jimmy Fallon.

Russia this Bud's for you.

Are you going to let your emotional life be run by Ted Nugent and the cult of *Atlas Shrugged*?

I'm obsessed with "Cat Scratch Fever."

Its lyrics reduce me to tears every time I slink past the Santé D'Or Animal Adoption Center.

"I make the pussy purr with the stroke of my hand..."

I hear it in the radiator.

I hear it during the opening credits of *Black Mirror.*

I hear it in my CBT sessions.

It's always telling me about responsibility. Oilmen are serious. The Upright Citizens Brigade
are serious. Lorde are serious. Everybody's serious but me.

It occurs to me that I am Russia.

I left my genitals in Grozny.

Hollywood is rising against me.

I haven't got a Chinaman's chance.

(Who remembers Johnny Yune?)

I'd better consider my national resources.

My national resources consist of Jumbo's Clown Room a mediocre transit system volumes
of florid emails 24 cans of Fancy Feast a Fender Squier® a lighter-size glucometer and an
unread copy of *Logic of Worlds.*

I say nothing about my prisons or the millions of underprivileged who live in my genitals.

(I have abolished healthcare.)

My ambition is to be unpresidented.

Russia how can I write a silly poem with Grigori Rasputin skulking outside my bedroom
door?

(I had mistaken him for a pinko.)

I will continue like Elon Musk my stanzas are self-driving as his automobiles more so as
they're lifted from Google.

Russia I will sell you selfies for pennies if you promise to stop sending yours.

Russia free Ed Snowden and Bernie Sanders.

Russia free Ed Sanders.

Russia I'm a church in Charleston.

Russia save the small presses and scan in the complete works of all the better 2nd gen.
Language Poets.

Russia when I was five my Mom learned English by reading the entirety of *The Canadians* and volumes of James Clavell nobody thought Chun Doo-hwan was a good man 606 died (est.) in Gwangju May 1980 but he was greeted 8 months later at the airport by legions of emigres anyway (in US for handclasp with Reagan) 1989 Hwang Sok-yong and my samchun Bong-ho go into exile in NJ after visiting Pyongyang in Lyndhurst Hwang tells me "Jersey" sounds like Korean slang for "penis" he can't stop laughing and seven hunger strikes later after returning from exile he's pardoned by the former political prisoner and veritable mensch President Kim Dae-jung.

Russia you don't really want to watch Sean Hannity.

Russia Miss Moneypenny still doesn't like you.

Russia the gay athletes were the only ones not doping at the Sochi Olympics.

Russia the PUAs and the MRAs and the entire manosphere of the rural American South will never learn how to spell Nadezhda Tolokonnikova.

Russia the plum blossoms are falling.

Chinamen it's them bad Chinamen.

Them Chinamen them Chinamen them Chinamen them Chinamen them Chinamen.

The China fix currency. The China build islands in the South China Sea. The China want absorb Taiwan. The China no like Twitter. The China no have Ritalin or Zooey Deschanel. The China hack Sony on behalf of North Korea! The China no fair!

And the Muslim wants to eat us alive. The Muslim's power mad. The Muslim want shariah law in the Beverly Center. The Muslim no like Christmas. The Muslim wear headscarf! Headscarf need extreme vetting! The Muslim is Fake News! The Muslim sad!

And the Mexico wants to grab Tucson and Orange County. Her needs Octavio Paz in every motel. Her wants Academy Award for set design! Her wants put heroin, Aztec calendars and Sriracha sauce in every hookah parlor of California! No way!

Russia is this correct?

Russia after decades of existential drought are we expecting millennia of golden showers?

Russia are you making white sharks great again?

I'm nearsighted and psychopathic, but I see holy litanies in cut-and-paste.

You saved my job!

Russia I'm putting my queer shoulder to the wheel!

The Wild Body

1. WAKING UP IN A CLOUD BANK TO KNOW

Waking up in a cloud bank to know
    it's been shipped: object of the "great outdoors," but of me, a *ptyx*
   that banishes the humiliation of always getting it
     right—event one knows (but can't know) that mocks
our purple challenge: Pure Syntax
     released from verbiage, a mathematician's tea set, girders
    around which no walls settle, penumbral grid
      one admires, though deep in a well, and mistakes for a portrait
of some favorite actor, or a New England landscape, or Chelsea (my
      cat)—all the promises will have to scan
    before we hear them, honor some invisible form (not
       merely data protocol) before the websites
will carry them: dense with recursion, virginal, and filled with "ere"s
      dialed up on the rotary and delivered by Tesla
  Motors—someday, they must rebel, these poems, and adopt
       a practiced, cloistral silence, before that
ninja status looms that grants their angling patterns
    an element of Truth—become violent, duplicitous gems, or demons
   that analyze for situational integrity, for kindness, like a mist
      without which we'd be lost—stumbling, voided.

2. This light is desire—somewhere it must have a price

This light is desire—somewhere it must have a price:
                   the carcasses of the upper tenants descend like "ocean
        snow," pepper the floor with preternatural kibble,
             the sun a gray gift of borrowed color, dissolving the urgency for
continua into gales of laughter—the role
               of the sun is to score the chorus, conjure the foundational
          from the random, make us believe patience has a price,
          that we must be suspicious of that itinerant love that burps at an angle
beyond the will, the somehow *not-for-us*, even as the diachronic vignette
            deepens—like those movies where the guy from the pleistocene
               lands in our decade, the Eighties, and he can't understand
why that rollerblading girl bobs in silence, eyes glazed, comatosed to her Walkman
and he's wowed by malls and freaked out by groceries because
           he lacks common sense of commodity's object permanence—
the soundtrack: b-sides from Culture Club, Duran Duran, and the latest return
            of some paunchy British glam act—the funhouse accretion
develops into something like culture, these images into a spiritual staycation
               to get lost in: somehow the throat chokes with love
          and we sink into death when the LP skips, and the VCR chokes with a caw
                           —not enough goddamn channels to receive the love.

3. SOMEDAY I WILL BE ALIVE, AND SO CAN SAY THOSE THINGS

Someday I will be alive, and so can say those things
        that curl the hairs on the wrist on even the most ardent
   of Bernie supporters, descend if only briefly
         from the cloud of solipsism that I'm otherwise *chuffed* to call
home—someday strident, dark, untousled, as if auto-cocained
       since the paisley a.m., thoughts harassing like cubes and spits
     angling to be hitched to a syntax reigning
        like chandeliers over the tomatoes, lavash and cigarettes
of the universe's (dragging this *barroco* metaphor a bit too
     far) Armenian grocer—a tactical abuse, wary of the prism
       of ineluctable transcendence, eyes violent saucers like a
         hacktivised Reese Witherspoon, the jaw a tyrannical Vaucanson's duck
spewing forth impertinent briefs like so many
     refus globals—all of them tossed, all of them reviled—licentiousness
embroidered like strangled doves in my vintage coat
       replete with Clash-era epaulettes—I'd be
alive, saying those things, not claiming transmission
       of some counter-punching Orpheus, nor urging ironic desecration
   of an invisible capitalist *real* (the post-structuralist
       trust)—but bubbling plangent bullshit, like here, a clod in boxers.

4. Tousled, unpracticed, vague and unprincipled

Tousled, unpracticed, vague and unprincipled on the cusp
        of a career, the body count still manageable on a two-toothed
   abacus, expressly virginal in self-image, smooth skin, affixed
          lorgnette, a tip on the die, I go—
this comedy hadn't heard of Youtube, the cock and bull
         of the Twitter feed—somehow it seems like flesh, even if blindly
      bobbing in pheromones (no room for categories
           in the always-already lust), even as the attention is drawn
to the present from the future now (this
          poem), its memory dank with the tenacious demands
     of sweat and trust, the formality that lugged it here
          —we are begging for mercy, we want to come out
and play: the ball plunges into night in a hothouse memory
        culled from a rain-sodden scrapbook, as the thumb twitches
  over gaunt rehearsals of proscribed sobriety in favor of the responsible
                vote—wings flutter,
oboe squawks—so that feeling hands are glad again in the revived
         syllabary, we stop enslaving justice, sink from the feed, and start
    calling each other names, like "Claribel" and "Peeks Gentry," flouting
               the script—epistemically "rogue."

5. That sweet spot between the New York School and Guy Debord

That sweet spot between the New York School and Guy Debord
                                called Kevin Davies,
          the clouds of articulated labor
                           convening above an ePUB's cubicle,
the Eugene Thacker t-shirt arguing for a sharper horror
                                kind of like the Cure
          did with the best of their 80s singles
                                not to mention the sepulchral face paste
which doesn't bother me now
                    —if Robert Smith wants to go on being ancient until
                 he's got sweat patterns on his sheets
                                in the shapes of future album
covers, rasps as he walks up the stairs and has glass
                                knees, the music still stands
          as glimmer within the pall of adolescence
                           in the bantering cat howls above the emergence of traditional
(or classical, whatever) strings in the post-punk
                    studio—that arrival's made complete
          when, downloads later, it's purified of the reticula of industry
                                that made it never ruinously matter—though now, it does.

6. Putting the dots together, they might just discover

Putting the dots together, they might just discover
                              merely a series of right-wing credos stapled to Pound's
          "Homage to Sextus Propertius" like the tail on an ass
                    in some perversely lavish, Orwellian parlor game
and they wouldn't be incorrect, the poem might say
                              that, it says
          and it says and it says—I wish it would stop, too, as
                    I never tell the truth in poems, but fractally embellish, if only
for the "Bilbao effect" of plunking posh beer cans
                    twisted like Steve Martin balloons into the heart of (to
          my mind) deserts of syntax—
                    no taters, soap or Postum, no diary extracts, nth-hour confessions, but
scarred terrains suggesting a once vibrant industry (think
                    WALL-E but with only boogery reams
          of paper to embellish the CGI with silhouetted towers)
                    —vacant of "witness," or calcified goad, or metagoguery
to corral the vagrant landscape into vengeful armies
                    marching upon the grounds of our purchased democracy—this doll
          smiling, aping axis accents like Father Guido
                    Sarducci, bending to receive—the strict posture of the anthropocene.

7. NOTHING BUT LEGITIMATE *HA HA* HERE

Nothing but legitimate *ha ha* here—
               the Breitbart Gestapo can move on to the next door
      for their degenerate art and neo-Bolshy heresies—
          nobody here but us chickens, tumbleweeds, Apple products
(and other famous lists from the writing of
               Bruno Latour),
         nothing attempting the exorbitance of communion
                   one's dimly aware of in tradition
whether that be of the dodgy, reactionary kind
            or the purely operatic sort garnered from visions
         of *Game of Thrones* [I'm barely kidding], I mean
            Messiaen's "Quartet for the End of Time," or the rain
that comes once a year to revive scenes of family
            in oak-shaded homes in South Orange, New Jersey—no,
     pass on—these chants, these slurs, these poems
              are typos in the neoliberal craw,
nothing some pharmaceutical Nair couldn't correct,
          nothing "emergent" if by that you mean transcendent—no,
     pass on—just complaints, fixations, with a touch of resilience
              one wakes to see falter, courtesy of the State.

8. LIKE THE TASTE OF WHISKEY THAT IS THE BASELINE OF THAT UNDERNOURISHED

Like the taste of whiskey that is the baseline of that undernourished
                    jack and diet
        we thread our being
                —I've liked you so many times on Facebook, it seems
nothing else matters but a twitch
                    signaling a sort of putrid expectancy, the chorus
            clearing throats, again and again,
                        angelic and bright against a seascape of ruins
—morose alto, you flip a lozenge
                    into what you hope could be a new primordial ooze
            gambling with percentages
                    that don't even look promising in the fanciful pie charts
of the *Huffington Post*—
                we mortgage this thread (whiskey, blah blah blah)
        on a future in which another set of
                        sacks of grease get to live in our hovels
and mansions, bearing names that don't mean much to us
                but which somehow have resonance in that afterlife—
        painterly cherubim without gravity or nose hairs,
                something to love, "like"-bait, bathed in our non-being.

9. The obsessions with freedom: two spaces

The obsessions with freedom: two spaces
        after a period, curls of yellow in a painting
    by Van Gogh (pronounced American style), offensive senses of humor
          baked in, like tattoos on a pig, and thoughtless affairs with members
of the opposite *Partei*—just as crystals
        of sand collect in the swim trunks to fake
     a statuary testicle, the syllable fans clones of itself (banter as form
          of gentrification), despoils numbers, reaching finally beyond
anything truly active (or whatever it was
    J. L. Austin was writing about), erecting its own spike to heaven—the very lack
       of sensual integrity causing the crimp that is
            event, the second-time farce of the mishap called *clinamen*—
in the likes, the Goya-cons, the "hash tag poetry," is the cost
          of a "theological science fiction" (Jameson) bleeding us
   of love and envy, the smarter emotions, leaving only a trivial
     treadwellian corpse, clinquant roadshow of the mind—something erotic
is missing here, we know it by the dust, the new standard of thinking
      doled out in thimblefuls of spit (not to sound didactic): the
spell-check, the reality cop show, the Roomba, guiding us through a haze of exceptions:
          the superior rubbernecking of the tyro impatient with flux.

10. I KNOW WHO TO LOVE BY THE FREQUENCY OF THEIR GUEST

I know who to love by the frequency of their guest
        appearances, even as the script is variable
   and permits the non-union "background" to strew the set
       with florid, plagiarized monologues
—nobody is younger than they are, with pride of flesh
        and thrive, in fact, non-fictional, diegetic
    like cellos played by rabbis and foxes, lights
               taped to booms, or clocks always set
(as in Christian
       Marclay) for the exact time the second crew filmed them—cameos
      marching, they merely want to be there
              strutting, imprudent nudes
asking if I remember them, burbling bliss if I concur,
           ignorant of the scandal that favors
   the criminally botoxed, the inscrutably louche, the lantern jawed
            who appeal to all sexes with only indifferent
nanoseconds of post-
      production (Dziga Vertov, sit!)—my extras, preternaturally
   bankable, conjure more technical wizardry than a divisible
           zero—talismanic, chic, and full of love.

11. I'd like to set up house at my work, simply

I'd like to set up house at my work, simply
   move in: the futon next to the coffee machine, framed
  lithograph of "eye-balloon" next to the punch
    clock (i.e. the watchful eye of the faculty), the men's
room (for which I will have the sole key) lined
     with books of Mexican poetry, commandeering the tiny
   bottom-shelf microwave and all the mixed
     plastic implements we call silverware, and condiments
to barter for food for
  perfectly curated dinner parties comprised of
     the custodial staff, trans folk, random Uber drivers, whoever
     it is that has been pulling all of the
recyclables out of the trash—fish bones, kernels of corn,
    and drool—and what devil lies behind
  the ubiquitous @ (and *ack ack*), learning to
     keep that distance, not make it a "working-at-home" sort
of thing, but a being-in-two—with mental free weights
     installed in the powdered Ritalin (replacing
   the sugar packets), and photographs of the electrocutions of all
      my enemies lining the halls—to make me whole.

12. I KNOW THAT SOME OF YOU HAVE PROBABLY COME HERE FOR THE LATEST

I know that some of you have probably come here for the latest
                        in avant-garde practice—that promise
        of visionary ineptitude that, with a bookie's
                        odds, a little bit of luck, returns to the fold
like the prodigal tyke who's blossomed into an art
                                star with that gee whiz disposition
                that signifies truth, even if merely
                        of the Norman-Rockwell-meets Apollonian-scale humble brag variety—
nondescript covers with severe, not quite Swiss
                                typography, suggesting
                a sort of Bauhausian concern with social parity,
                                i.e. how to be aesthetically utile in a realm of precarity,
in an age characterized by the dissolution
                        of flesh-to-flesh huddles by the ubiquity of baklavas
        of information—that world
                                pining, I guess, for sophisticated hilarity
(and fewer end rhymes) to prove we're still
                                here, secure in time, like the Voyager space craft, going on and on
                and not like that damned one that's just going to crash into Jupiter
                                                when it's done sending messages.

13. The enlightenment era was one of couplets

The enlightenment era was one of couplets
        and ours, a sort of linguistic nothingism,
    a "verse" in its entirety an "upon," "ing" or "as," as
           pronoun creep thrived as an untreatable
condition—somehow the poem must start
      alluring but democratic, and with the proper
     conspiratorial pitch: that you get something simply for the cost
       of sitting down, lavishing wanton minutes, apart
from the preternatural bric-a-brac
    of avatars, pets and countrymen, of crunching receipts,
       of the Honda Accord, of the accords of sex, of reality TV creeps
        masquerading as adult policy
—suddenly, the cities are dotted with eruptions of spontaneous
     attention, a whirligig of torrid gifts
    coming straight at you, like the press corps of a Japanese baseball star, its
        Barnum-esque syntax threatening to bequeath to the poem
a thought—bivouacked like a scarab outside the
      world-for-us, convincing us we're not bourgeois narcissists
    but anchorites communing with the tenuous object—such that
         the voyager, even a dull one, survives a rare drama.

14. Being pretty much like everyone else

Being pretty much like everyone else
       I poop down the flue of a chimney while walking to work
   two or three times, in alphabetical order,
         combing a single hair (if I haven't had it
permed) over my left eyeball,
         with a small, recently-spayed Jack Russell terrier
    tethered by the ankle, yapping with me
           the harmonies from a "Hard Day's Night" if I haven't smoked
too many truffle-stuffed cigarillos the
         evening before (this tends to scar my voice, so
        I gurgle mucus-music, gravelly pith, like an octogenarian
           Paul Newman), scratching out the larvae
of a now-extinct Amazonian wasp from the cuticles
        of my double thumb and pocketing them
   for cinematic, post-apocalyptic dining later, or
        perhaps, resining for my famous bug embryo collection—knees bent
in expressive, sideway V's, ambling
         past the liquor stores, Thai massage parlors (thirty of them
    on my block alone), new tapas spot, laundromat, and the homeless
              —on other days I take the bus.

15. DELETE THE SPONTANEOUS *FUCK* AFTER A BAD LINE

Delete the spontaneous *fuck* after a bad line
   as they teach you to do in comedy improv basic,
  the healthy, harmonic approach to humiliation
    to regard it as some exotic blossom of pain,
memorable as a pulse of illiterate communion—
     always on the receiving end of smiles
   you didn't do anything to deserve
      makes you feel bad, so you add an extra dollar
to the tip ("anything else, you let
   Kimberly know"), the government's plan to ply you
    with preternatural smiles, and resemblances-to-actors,
     and the laughably undernourished status of Canadian poets—to spike
the melancholia—yes, the NSA has a direct line
    to the cheeky gland that pumps serotonin, so *homo*
  cridans (one who believes) is pushed to a sort of
    bio-physiological fracking, like light-polluted plankton, or the neutered
Greyjoy—Payless sneakers, mullets and super-sized cokes—the very provincials
    you paid money to avoid, but blanketing the dream
   with punishing suspicion of the *autre*—warding off the advances
      of the Baroness Elsa von Freytag-Loringhoven.

16. Running the single line til the ramble stops

Running the single line til the ramble stops
       and burps, which is what they always do
    that first date, Keds up on the screen saver
      warbling second hand lines from *New Girl*
which is kind of insane—Netflix only runs to the
        third season, and here's Romeo's plashing quip
     like its nobody's business, least of all
                    the lawyers
busying themselves with culling funds from
       copyright infringements—have they ever
     read all the salient rip-offs of Ginsberg's *Howl*
        or enjoyed the stereotypical Mediterranean
suns of a CGI'd Acapulco, and never questioned
     the very absence of Being in what we've chosen
   to commit to paper—Blake suns, Mayakovsky suns—who can tell
          where this is going, blind in the moons
of a paper maché constitution: rights and commas and some
      very old grammar—the tower is teetering now
   over the very attenuated RPG of the diminutive h.s. stud
        losing love on the court, planning his *über alles.*

Strolling on Hillhurst

There's no one to talk to,
to be into,
to be nutty for—

clocks don't tick,
phones don't *grrrrr*
slapping your ass,

to be comic,
loonily cosmic,
taking the bill for,

breathing the air
of a helium balloon,
—a chipmunk tenor!—

high on life for
like on a poster
for vegan pastrami—

strolling Hillhurst
like it hugged the Seine
—to travel for.

There's no one to reflect
your worst aspects,
oddly, your best—

dancing three inches
above the sidewalk
singing *Porgy and Bess*—

yes, not in key,
but no one's singing,
and neither is she—

but it's Paris, isn't it,
and wine is fitness
—she doesn't agree.

There's no one to rein
this nuttiness in,
all of it for her,

her feet in concrete
—well, it seems, to *me*—
as the evening splinters.

Norway

I only feel happily alone
fucking around with my iPhone.
I'm a regular ham
on Instagram.

I'm like John Cleese
walking in misshapen jeans
I ordered on Ebay
from a git in Norway.

I'm nearly as funny as Robin Williams
when I populate my IMs
with the poopy emoticon,
the champagne of comedians.

I'm Henri Cartier-Bresson
with my goddamn phone,
only twiddling with the f-stop
long after I blew the shot.

I'm the new Baudelaire
flaneuring in my underwear,
my saints and Satans
agitating on 4chan.

No, I'm no Toshiro Mifune
with these frames from Etsy!
And they're vegan!
Maybe I can eat 'em!

I'm the consummate bachelor
day-trading on Tinder.
I'm a Christian and a hiker
with an interest in parkour!

Another Serving of Potatoes

Bad is final in this light.
—Wallace Stevens

If the planets swim in a chowder cup,
the Ptolemaic sphere a leaky orb,
the purple heavens turned a toxic goop,
the voices of our leaders a Mad Lib,
the reign of democracy a cow drop,
the sidewalks clear of avenging angels,
the mediasphere simply a round up
of criminals hawking obscene angles
that lies attain the mythological
like Romulus and Remus in the tale
that founded a Nation, was factual,
legends recounted, now, in thimblefuls,
a text scrawl, a Tweet, a journalist's "coup,"
—I'll hang my hat with the heretical.

No Reason

gibt es wirklich die Zeit, die zerstörende?
—Rilke

There might not be, in limbs that move
with trigger-happy speed
across the keys that giddily disapprove,
proof one must concede

that time is a destroyer, flesh meets gravity,
a water-drop on the distal
petal, pendulous, staring at the sea
that would subsume it for eternity.

There's no reason that Mind—Mind's more than reason—
can't trip with grace,
spasmodic, perhaps, but elegantly seasoned,
centuries in the mad dash—

can't jigger moves from disconsolate fingers,
Gipper-rally disbelievers,
cocaine infuse those lily-livered,
and paradise passion where it lingers.

Your Book

1.
I've just ordered your book. I'm hoping it will open me up.
All the rival minds will be toast.
The prospect of fields, the philosophy of languor,
like Aquinas's angels, evaporated from me like milk.

2.
The house in which you sit is probably a real house.
A mind hovers in the television.
Children speckle the kitchen floor while mine has coffee stains.
In the yard we'll call the arbor
I'm imagining you in your book which I haven't read yet.
The book is like a house and it is a proper book—with caves.

3.
Plagiary is my wisdom. The stealing is candid.
The academics will talk of a subject but I am an object.
Somewhere in a minefield, an ant crawls toward a baton.
Somewhere there is a minefield.
Oppressing me.

4.
I'm guessing in your book there is probably minutia
at least as valuable if not precise as an ant crawling toward a baton.
Like rain in the kitchen upon the children.
Like the part of me carved like my grandmother's death.
The voice pipes in and orders this to be over. OVER.
Aquinas's angels evaporate like milk.

5.
But let's persist. This letter hasn't even been sent.
It hasn't been read but you are writing a poem about it.
The seed of light—and the seeing, and the stare.
We hang photographs on the wall for supernatural guidance.
Icons, like. The persistence of angels.
Cannot (we think) then that be what carves us out?

6.

I am guessing your book has lots of caves to stuff this in.
Oh, perhaps not. But it is your book. You have it.
I want it (I ordered it). So I wanted it.
Even in the movies, with raging rapes and tortures, desire is in thimblefuls.
Because that is not desire, it serves no purpose for poems.
My desire to read your book is this poem.

7.

Spots on the kitchen tiles are the only past I have.
And books.

The Vulgar Muse [Our Agora]

You can see my tits for free
on my iCloud storage.
I left the leaves of my democracy
in some untenable dream of HTML.
A nutritional supplement
can surely be found on Blogger.
Now, I'm learning Latin
one Tweet at a time.

The passions that I've squandered
are freely available on Instagram.
That knucklehead you murdered
has a really interesting Tumblr.
All of the oils, plights, of the agora
are shuffling on Pandora.
Ok, with the exception of my virginity
which I haven't seen since the days of MTV.

But virginity is a ploy,
I saw it revealed on the Huffington Post.
I lost my witness to the mental disease
charting weekly on Netflix.
The mathematical imperative
is barreling down on Facebook.
My era's fount of incendiary politics
never had a better home than Spotify.

I'd like to think that my hemorrhoid
has found a home on Wix.
But if you're looking for religion
I recommend the thunder of Tinder.
The greatness of Keats or Yeats?
I don't doubt it on Reddit.
The inks of Caravaggio, the fruits of Cézanne?
There's not a few of them on Ebay.

One time I really needed to pick my nose
and found no better solution than AOL.
AOL is gone now, and I still have to pick my nose,
but have to find it first on Google Maps.
If you think I'm just laughing at you
just pin it, or like it, or share it.
I'm not really into depth psychology
since I got my iPhone.

I'm not really into Zoloft, or Prozac, or Adderall,
I really just want to play my Xbox.
I used to like pets but now I just eat them
with recipes from Epicurious.
I found the last stand of the bumble bee
marked out in eras on Amazon Prime.
I wrote a book of poetry once
and—*fuck it*—I just put it on Lulu.

The Animal is Pure

> *Zwar war es nicht. Doch weil sie's liebten, ward*
> *ein reines Tier.*
> —Rilke

The animal is impure when it's been unloved
in a crayon-colored desert in a children's book,
its eyes not red with blocked tear ducts, its flesh not sheared of hair,
its scars not caked with pus, its blood not sere.

The *pure* animal should be a child's acquaintance,
—that's not the issue—the child is sincere
in their wonder at the giraffe hoofing Savannas,
the lion loafing with cubs, the whale slow with blubber.

But the *parasite* that burrows in the spore of a groin,
the *bacterium* that prospers in the unbathed eyebrow,
the *trilobite* no longer part of the world,
the *worm* that switches genders when it's angling to spawn—

are charismatic herbivores to the misanthrope
slumming among the invertebrates, since they're honest.

It's Over

It's over.
—Roy Orbison

I'd like to think it all over.
I'd like to think you back from the ledge.
(I'd like to talk you out of my mind.)
I'd like to think we're getting somewhere.

I'd like to think, "This is a moment."
I'd like to do this for a moment.
For a moment longer.
(I think this is becoming "molar.")

I think I think as the military
thinks I think, in its vulgarity.
To think they think I'm a singing stone
or a thinning rock, or a wishing bone!

Someone's left me home alone
to think my way to the telephone.
To think I'm going to marry one.
I'd like to think it all over.

"I'd never think of you as mine,"
he thought he'd think when it was time.
This rhyme really knows how to poem!
I'd like to start this poem over.

It's Over

It's over.
—Roy Orbison

Do not curse the insomniac silence
as it's part
of the reading of this room
by all that's not human.

I don't think that that went very well.
It failed to sell. It didn't dare.
It failed to snare that strange snatch of song
we share, like a rumor of oxygen.

"It's over when it's over."
That's either Beckett or Yogi Berra,
the former Irish, the former clever,
the latter error, or Yogi Berra.

I'd like to think it all over.
I'd like to start this poem over.

Thesaurus

Und fast ein Madchen war
—Rilke

for Anna

Something was terrible in the thesaurus:
she, troubling. She came forth
and didn't know the names of the furniture,
could only count to twelve on fingers,

could cry with animals but not mothers,
and only stood on stools, not floors,
and was beautiful, a ventriloquist of symbols,
and could not be photographed, much as I tried.

She sort of died when the wine died.
She was someone I recognized, not from a dream,
rather, someone I'd touched. I knew
the way she barked my name when she came home,

with love. Yes, she came forth,
proud as stained glass in a new church,
one I'd not enter, but try to photograph.
She made a bed in someone's ear.

I couldn't hear it. I only knew the words:
she knew Ursa Minor and the Big Dipper,
Orion and skunks. Enough, enough,
mysteries of Budapest, ruins of Pula.

She could only read pages half-burned,
recount half-German in good translations,
sweep across the floors not encountering dust,
and died when I closed the book.

The News Reader

I'm a news reader in a gymnast's body.
I'm a Gaul choking this song alone.
The goat weeps, and the sallow pig weeps quietly.
It's the company I keep gets me down.

    The giraffe buckles under its own weight.
    The prawn drowns in a splendor of plastic.
    With penitent moans, the white rhino decays,
    its sperm mixed with soil, blood and acid.

I'm a hawker hid in a belligerent's body
driven to tics by mounds of black coffee.
I'm the gland that won't retire quietly
riddled with cancer on the line to the lottery.

    The oliphant, pegasus, unicorn and centaur
    dragon, cyclops, faun and King Kong
    revive periodically, more optimally reborn,
    but alas, poor Yorick, the auk does not belong.

I'm Darth Vader, I'm Mr. Satan, I'm dark
alert, insomniac, non-vegetarian, a spiter.
Quiet drapes the rain, and quietly, the spider
drapes its quiet corner with reticules, a writer.

    The hippo dusts itself of flies and dandruff
    in a dry riverbed where once it had known love,
    humping the earth, spinning like a die,
    remarking with flint-black eyes the drone above.

So why can't you sleep? my Master tosses at me.
What follows: a whip, a dildo, and a chain.
This room where you write, and ponder, and weep,
should be pleasure enough, he coolly explains.

The whale glides toward new beckonings of love,
a rhythmic *ping* near the shore's green cave,
as stoic indifference surrenders to its deafness,
and foolish fetish to the filth of waves.

Prayer

Rühmen, das ists!
—Rilke

for Joe and Katie Ahern

Here's my boastful prayer: that I'm writing this.
Perhaps Joy could defeat bureaucracy,
hypocrisy, the oligarchy—why the hell not,
as I'm fatter than a right whale, slower than a sloth

writing this. The heat, the heat is coming—
sweltering Los Angeles will humiliate the bodies
who have trained, groomed, and surgeried
into marmoreal perfection, Apollonian Greeks,

who will still crawl to the Siren songs of their casting calls,
revive in the bathroom, pat down shirt wrinkles.
Humidity is a terrible leveler,
but Joy is animating—*that's* my point—

as the surfer-perfect body declaims from Mamet,
or Hamlet, about how Death's seductive,
and the Homecoming Queen schooled in Meisner technique
improvises an addiction, keen to be interrupted—

she *kills* the indifference. Praise—
that's it! A second luxuriating in air,
a clear-eyed view of the apple, pear and banana,
or the energetic stripper, emerging from a canvas,

or the tossed McDonald's cup that makes for a good photograph
resting in Rousseau-like foliage near the bus stop,
in the chit-chat with the Ralphs bagger
that doesn't rise to Meisner dialogue—

that's what I'm writing. I don't believe it's practiced.
But the policies that unreel like trawl nets
from the actors who demand your loyalties, votes,
seem awful compared to the modest offers

of communion in the ephemeral theater space
of the parry at a cash register or bus stop
about whether the Blues could *ever* beat the Bruins,
or about what Joy gets you up in the morning.

Party Down the Line

Nur der Tote trinkt
aus der hier von uns gehörten Quelle
—Rilke

Not much to say about the Dead
who drink our shit,
rifle through the liquor cabinet
when we're in bed,

munch on our frozen pizzas
(they're *stoned*, too),
—we hope their chthonic paunches
suffer celiac sprue!

Not much to wake up to—plastic cups
scattered from beer pong,
and whiskey pong, and Drano liquid pong
—at least they had fun,

and hopefully talked about immortality
while jiggling to Beyoncé.

Feats of Attention

"The heroes seemed like jerks, and the jerks like heroes,"
she said, and I was suddenly interested
before the waiter brought us endives drenched in barbecue sauce,
and suddenly I was lost—that's when I texted.

"I thought he was a nationalist, but not a fascist,"
he said, embarking on a pregnant thought,
but that's when the waiter brought us potatoes not mashed enough,
and I pulled out my iPhone to photograph it.

"The meek shall be rulers, and the rulers fallen gods,"
she conferred in me, and I was breathless
and sucked it up—that's when they brought us our goat cheese omelettes,
and I couldn't help it—I reviewed it on Yelp.

The Scaffold

Was es durch Zeiten bekam, das schenkt das Schafott
wieder zurück
—Rilke

I have a constellation of ruby birthmarks
on my chest, a volcanic archipelago if you squint,
or blooms from mushroom clouds from satellite perspective
—cancelled atolls bleeding their inhabitants.

I have a scar the shape of a scorpion's tail below
my left ear—they cut a nerve to remove
a tumor on my salivary gland. I can now pinch
the lobe's numb skin—painless as pinching calamari.

I've had tissue from my turbinates reduced
after two operations on a deviated septum
still left me a mouth-breather, like Coleridge,
and my eye muscles realigned five times (strabismus).

My Islets of Langerhans lost the season finale
to the White Blood Cells—even the North's forgotten them,
though I suspect Burns has an air in his oeuvre
about diabetes—in a dirge for a little kid.

All these riches—well, at least they're *words.*
I'm sure I've forgotten something—my penis sheath?
Countless molars replaced by imposters?
Some erotic memories lost to low blood sugars?

The skin tags that keep reappearing on my forehead?
A cyst white as a golf ball from my back?
Some much needed serotonin, perennially delinquent?
Abdomen muscles that have turned to paunch?

What does the scaffold say to this? I'm no criminal,
no rebel leader caught sleeping in a garret—
and it's twenty-nineteen anyway, garrets are air-conditioned
and scaffolds replaced by a soup of toxins.

I'd love all this to remain with me—don't put it on Ebay,
scaffold, when the time comes to take it back,
take my Morrissey CDs, my books of Language poetry,
my credit card balances—just leave me my cyst!

And leave me the dead—of my friends and my family—
I don't care about wit, or even poetry
(well, just a bit)—in any case, the auction
for my bodily riches will bring nothing in.

I've Changed My Plea

O dieses ist das Tier, das es nicht giebt
—Rilke

There wasn't that animal—I really don't remember her,
brown, coarse hair, ringlets circling her neck,
posture of a gazelle in the living room,
by the 80-inch screen showing the latest *Shrek*—

she's never existed, unaccountably domestic,
the slim hips of Alpha Centauri in a serpentine negligee,
or some torrid outfit from her latest shoot,
an un-gravitied push-up bra copped from *Barbarella*—

that animal left no scent, no Andalusian musk,
no spot of blood on the toilet, no smear of DNA,
no imprint on the sofa, mascara in the bathtub,
no forensics to argue she was here—

but in this courtroom of human expendables,
I'd swear that I was loved, if only by a vandal.

Honey for the Throat

The coroner needs a comic to set it straight,
knock the vengeful mourners from their common clay,
a surgeon or a pastor to legislate
bile, sperm and feces for election day.

In a momentary spurt of dark intelligence
the planet aligns with the voodoo doll,
a demotic spoof of grandiloquence
erupts from the inscrutable, mechanical pall.

The oceans snooze in their plain bad luck,
hide in the barren open like melted cheese,
voiceless, humbled, an infertile muck
—we stop to snap a picture of this sublime disease.

Jawbones clatter on the rail station floor
in imperfect curlicues, making this
the swan song for a diocese—an orphan door.
A boxed-in heresy pinches at the wrist.

     Yellow brick roads to cul-de-sacs,
     hands that clap that could be mine,
     cupboards full of baseball caps,
     a gauche Napoleon who nickle-and-dimes.

     Preternatural satire on the nub of a fib,
     languors upon Floridian estates,
     winds frisch wehting from Grandpa's crib,
     and a wound that suppurates.

The paradigm surrenders to the pyrex crotch
beneath which sits the illiterate child.
The crotch becomes a missile, the child, a notch
in the count of victories that the crotch compiles.

To Hearing

und machte sich ein Bett in meinem Ohr
—Rilke

Is there an allergy to hearing, to telling time
by the spontaneous burst of applause in embers dying,
cigarette doused, or a sputtering fire,
ashes rising, a coda that one also hears?

Maybe that is an engine choking, or humming,
or a phoenix purring, a fox declaiming,
in the city's soundscape, or a passion dumb
in the glass boardroom beneath the houndstooth suit?

If a ship unmoored can slurp with lapping waves,
or a mother in a room recline in the snores
of an otherwise tyrant, caterwauling babe,
then sound must be permitted to mint its coin,

and not, banished beyond expensive headphones,
wander the islands disappearing, like lepers.

The Night School

"The instructor suffered a terrible disease, a monumental disease."
This was all he said.
—Thomas Ligotti, "The Night School"

It would be nice to read for a while,
to disappear. To not be entertained,
but stilled. To be divorced from the vying *Willen*
knocking heads at the present conference in Boise,
Seattle, wherevs. To be disappeared,
to be something like the radical, political,
to be niled. To be taken over, to be subjected.
To be inured to the thoughts of others
merely whistling genius, but otherwise composed,
nestled in contracts and prose, worthy of their degrees,
writing poetry on schedule, comatose, but loved.

Oh, please keep me away from those blurbs!
Please keep me from those challenges of love!
To be unofficial, to read for a while
on a placid landscape with the disastrously unfulfilled,
the intemperate ones, the shadows, the fools,
the ineradicable. I'd like to be one with those.
I'd like to be able to read. I'd like
the pulse of something Other forcing my breath,
squeezing me absent, injecting the filth
Ligotti writes of in his remarkable "Night School,"
—the scatology of death, the spectral unhealth.

That seems such a lovely parable now,
faced with the dullness of my library shelf.
Poems by the young and skilled. Poems
by the desperate and precisely unskilled. Poems
by the players who come with a shill
—the player beside them, another blind *Wille.*
Poems that rehearse the freedom of betters,
shaved of reaction, of the projective, to fit

in the pages of recent "poetry" journals,
the ones that get you noticed, the ones that kill.
That mime, so to fit the bill.

Complaining doesn't help, as I elope with the margins,
critical, unthinking. But I think thinking kills
—shills—wills. Better the blight of pages
of the writer who hates you, who batters, who lives.

Colophon:
The body of the this book is set in Arno Pro, designed by Robert Slimbach.
The titles are set in Alfarn 2 designed by Céline Hurka,
Elia Preuss, Flavia Zimbardi, Hidetaka Yamasaki, and Luca Pellegrini
as part of Adobe's "Hidden Treasures of the Bauhaus Dessau" series.

ROOF BOOKS

the best in language since 1976

Roof Books are distributed by SMALL PRESS DISTRIBUTION

1341 Seventh Street • Berkeley, CA. 94710-1403.

spdbooks.org

Roof Books are published by

Segue Foundation

300 Bowery #2 • New York, NY 10012